AIR
POLLUTION

Darren Sechrist

Marshall Cavendish
Benchmark

New York

Marshall Cavendish Benchmark
99 White Plains Road
Tarrytown, NY 10591
www.marshallcavendish.us

Library of Congress Cataloging-in-Publication Data

Sechrist, Darren.

   Air pollution / by Darren Sechrist

   p. cm. -- (Saving our world)

   Includes bibliographical references and index.

   ISBN 978-0-7614-3220-3

 1. Air--Pollution--Juvenile literature. I. Title.

   TD883.13.S43 2008

   363.739'2--dc22

   2008014833

The photographs in this book are used by permission and through the courtesy of:

Half Title : Juliengrondin/Shutterstock; Oleg Prikhodko/Istockphoto.

Roza/ Dreamstime: 4-5, ExaMedia Photography/Shutterstock: 7, 2007 American Honda Motor Co., Inc.: 8-9, Juliengrondin/Shutterstock: 10-11, Mike Goldwater / Alamy: 12-13, Getty Images: 14-15, Associated Press: 17, Pedro Luz Cunha / Alamy: 18-19, Kenneth M Highfill/Photolibrary: 20, Associated Press: 23, Millan/Bigstock: 25, Bill Bachmann / Alamy: 26-27, Otmar Smit/Shutterstock: 29

Cover photo: Sharply_done / Istockphoto; Debibishop / Istockphoto.

Illustrations : Q2A Media Art bank.

Created by: Q2A Media

Creative Director: Simmi Sikka

Series Editor: Maura Christopher

Series Art Director: Sudakshina Basu

Series Designers: Dibakar Acharjee, Joita Das, Mansi Mittal, Rati Mathur and Shruti Bahl

Photo research by Sejal Sehgal

Series Illustrators: Ajay Sharma and Abhideep Jha

Series Project Managers: Ravneet Kaur and Shekhar Kapur

Printed in Malaysia

1 3 5 6 4 2

CONTENTS

What Is Air Pollution?

Even though you can't see it, the air is an important resource. When the air gets polluted, or dirty, it can cause many serious problems. Keeping the air clean keeps people, animals, and the environment healthy.

Gases given off by cars and trucks can damage air quality and can also affect global temperatures.

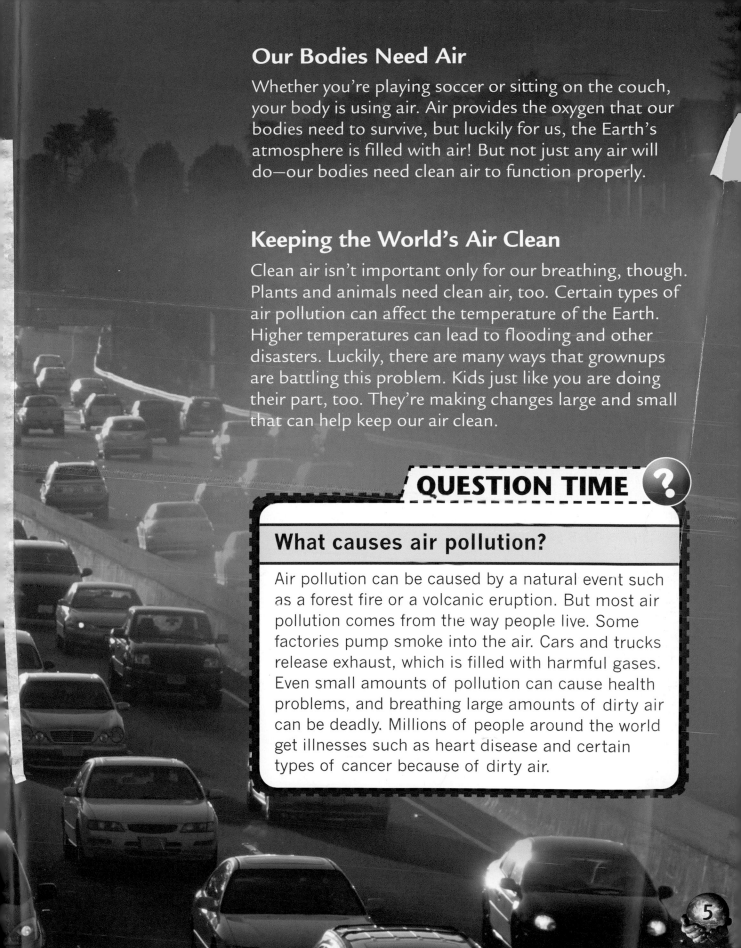

Our Bodies Need Air

Whether you're playing soccer or sitting on the couch, your body is using air. Air provides the oxygen that our bodies need to survive, but luckily for us, the Earth's atmosphere is filled with air! But not just any air will do—our bodies need clean air to function properly.

Keeping the World's Air Clean

Clean air isn't important only for our breathing, though. Plants and animals need clean air, too. Certain types of air pollution can affect the temperature of the Earth. Higher temperatures can lead to flooding and other disasters. Luckily, there are many ways that grownups are battling this problem. Kids just like you are doing their part, too. They're making changes large and small that can help keep our air clean.

QUESTION TIME ?

What causes air pollution?

Air pollution can be caused by a natural event such as a forest fire or a volcanic eruption. But most air pollution comes from the way people live. Some factories pump smoke into the air. Cars and trucks release exhaust, which is filled with harmful gases. Even small amounts of pollution can cause health problems, and breathing large amounts of dirty air can be deadly. Millions of people around the world get illnesses such as heart disease and certain types of cancer because of dirty air.

How and Where

There are many types of air pollution. They can be solids, liquids, or gases. Some types are more common in cities, while others can exist anywhere.

Specks in the Air

There are different types of air pollution. One of the most common types is **particulate matter**—tiny bits of harmful materials that get mixed in with the air. Some of these are solid, including ash, dust, and harmful metals such as lead. Some are liquid such as sprays and mists.

EYE-OPENER

Smoggy Cities/Clean Cities
Air pollution is a particular problem in big cities such as Mexico City. In part because the city has so many cars and trucks, many of the city's residents have respiratory, or breathing problems caused by the pollution.

ALASKA
Anchorage
Great Falls
Bismarck
Cheyenne
Detroit
Cleveland
Pittsburgh
Indianapolis
Visalia
Bakersfield
St. Louis
Cincinnati
Los Angeles
Farmington
Santa Fe
Flagstaff
Albuquerque
Tucson
Birmingham

MEXICO

Mexico City

- U.S. and Mexican metropolitan areas with most year-round particulate air pollution
- U.S. cities with the least long-term particulate air pollution

Source: The American Lung Association, 2007

6

Harmful Gases

Another type of air pollution occurs when harmful gases mix with the air. Many harmful gases, such as **carbon monoxide**, are created when **fossil fuels** are burned. Fossil fuels are burnable materials, such as oil or coal, that are the remains of living things found in the ground. Other harmful gases, like **radon**, can come from natural sources.

Seeing Is Believing?

Some of the worst types of pollution are created when harmful gases and solids mix with the air. Smoke from burning wood is an example. You can see smoke, but most pollutants are difficult to detect without special instruments. The deadly gas carbon monoxide cannot be seen or smelled. That's why many people have carbon monoxide detectors in their homes.

Coal plants like this one emit harmful gases into the air.

Pollution from People

Human activities are a major source of air pollution. Our cars, trucks, and other forms of transportation do a great deal to pollute the air.

Pollution from Cars and Trucks

Cars and trucks are a leading human cause of air pollution in the United States and around the world. When they burn gasoline or diesel (both fossil fuels), some of the fuel is released into the air as **exhaust**. These leftover ingredients include soot, carbon monoxide, and other materials that are harmful to our air.

Hybrid cars, like this Honda Civic, put fewer pollutants in the air.

Millions of Cars

The exhaust from a single car or truck does not have much effect on the air's cleanliness. But there are now more than 200 million vehicles in the United States alone. Countries such as China and India are becoming more reliant on cars, too. All of that exhaust adds up, especially in cities where many cars are packed into small areas.

Cleaner Cars

In recent years, people have started to demand cars that pollute less. In response, car companies have started making cleaner cars. Some of these are simply very **fuel efficient** gasoline-powered cars. Others are **hybrids**—vehicles that are partially powered by electricity, reducing their use of gasoline. Companies are also working on electric, solar, and other types of cars that create little or no exhaust.

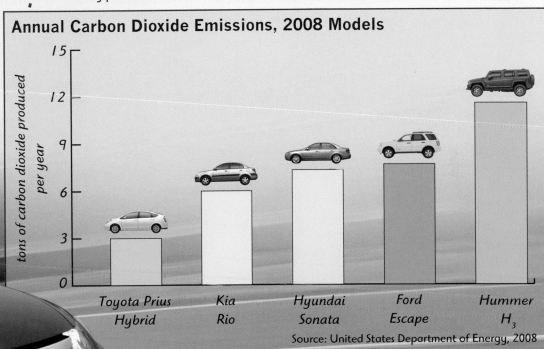

Annual Carbon Dioxide Emissions, 2008 Models

tons of carbon dioxide produced per year

| | Toyota Prius Hybrid | Kia Rio | Hyundai Sonata | Ford Escape | Hummer H_3 |

Source: United States Department of Energy, 2008

Other Polluting Vehicles

Cars and trucks are not the only forms of transportation that cause pollution. Airplanes burn hundreds of gallons of jet fuel during takeoff and while maintaining their speed in the air. Trains, boats, buses, and other vehicles also pump harmful gases and solids into the air. Luckily, walking and bicycling are still clean options!

Natural Pollution Everywhere

Cars and trucks are not the only causes of air pollution. Many other sources, both humanmade and natural, can do serious damage to the air.

When a volcano erupts, it can pump large amounts of ash and harmful gases into the air.

Factories and the Air

Some factories cause pollution when they make the products that we use every day. When plastics are created, chemicals are released into the air. The making of metal goods, paper, and other products creates harmful gases that find their way into the air.

Nature's Air Pollution

Naturally occurring forest fires can fill the air with smoke and ash. Radon, which is a harmful gas, is found in the ground and can build up in the basements of people's homes. When volcanoes erupt, they blast gases and ash into the air. An eruption of Mount Tamboro (near Indonesia) in 1815 put so much dust into the air that it affected temperatures around the world.

Bringing Air Pollution Home

Running our homes, offices, and other buildings contributes to air problems, too. Many of these buildings are heated by the burning of oil or other fossil fuels. They also use electricity to run machinery, to power appliances or electronics, and to provide light. In most places, electricity is created by burning coal and other fossil fuels or through an energy source called **nuclear power**. Both of these methods create dirty air.

QUESTION TIME ?

Are any buildings good for the environment?

Yes. Today, people are trying to construct buildings that pollute less. Building cleaner structures prevents air pollution and saves energy costs. Some homes, factories, and offices are now **zero-emissions buildings**. This means that they don't pump any pollution into the air at all.

Air Pollution Harm

Air pollution can cause a number of health problems. Respiratory, or breathing, diseases are one common type. Unclean air has also been linked to heart problems and many types of cancer.

Airway Illnesses

Millions of people around the world suffer from a respiratory disease called **asthma**. People with asthma have airways that become inflamed, or swollen. When air pollution or other irritating materials enter the airways, they can trigger an asthma attack. The muscles of the airway tighten up, making it very difficult to breathe. In a severe attack, the airway may close so much that little or no oxygen makes it into the body. A very severe asthma attack can be deadly. People with asthma use devices called **inhalers** to help clear their airways.

In coal mines, workers can breathe in tiny specks of coal dust. This can lead to serious health problems.

High-Risk Breathing

In some places, air pollution is a bigger risk than in others. People who work in coal mines, for instance, are in danger of breathing harmful coal dust and getting a disease called "black lung." Those who work with metals can get very sick from the vapors that are created when metals are heated. Construction workers may breathe in the cancer-causing fibers of **asbestos**, a material used in an old form of insulation. These workers all have to use protective equipment to limit their exposure to these dangerous materials.

EYE-OPENER

Asthma is a growing problem in the United States. The following graph shows how the number of cases of asthma has increased since 1980.

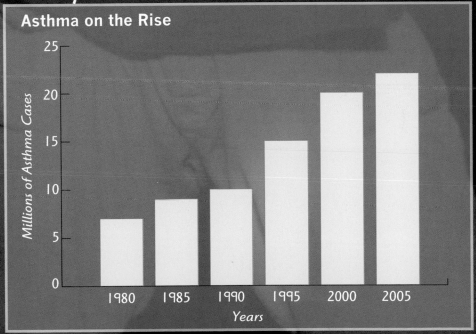

Asthma on the Rise

Millions of Asthma Cases vs. *Years*

Sources: For 1980 to 1995 data: D.M. Mannino, D.M. Homa, C.A. Pertowski, A. Ashizawa, L.L. Nixon, C.A. Johnson, L.B. Ball, E. Jack, D.S. Kang.
Surveillance for asthma - United States, 1960–1995. Morbidity and Mortality Weekly Report 47 (SS-1): 1–27 (1998). For 2000 to 2005 data:
National Health Interview Survey, National Center for Health Statistics, CDC.

Air Pollution Disasters

Air pollution is usually a long-term problem. Harmful materials slowly build up in the air over years and years. But sometimes air pollution can strike quickly and cause an instant disaster.

Children run through the streets of Bhopal, India, just days after a deadly poisonous gas leak in 1984.

Deadly Air in Donora, Pennsylvania

As early as 1918, the people in and around Donora, Pennsylvania, noticed that air pollutants from the local metal and chemical plants were affecting their health and damaging their crops. Residents considered the murky air an inconvenience, but not a serious risk. In 1948 that changed quickly. That October, a warm air mass prevented the plants' hazardous **emissions** from escaping into the upper atmosphere, as they normally would. A toxic cloud of sulfur dioxide, carbon monoxide, and metal dust settled over the town of 14,000 people. Over the next five days, twenty people died and another 7,000 were sickened. The disaster drew national attention to the problem of air pollution.

London Smog Disaster

London, England, is famous for its thick fog, and London residents have long burned coal to heat their homes. The mix creates a constant **smog** (a combination of smoke and fog). But a period of unusually cold weather in December 1952 led Londoners to burn more coal than ever. The result was an incredibly thick, dark cloud of smog. Drivers could not see. Schools were closed. Thousands of people, many already weakened by the usual air pollution, died from respiratory problems. In all, an estimated 12,000 were killed. In response, the British government passed its first air pollution laws in 1956.

The Bhopal Gas Leak

Shortly after midnight on December 3, 1984, the Union Carbide pesticide plant in Bhopal, India, began leaking **methyl isocyanate**. Twenty-seven tons of the deadly gas escaped and spread through the city. The disaster killed 2,500 people and made hundreds of thousands of others sick. The chemical company was ordered to pay $470 million to the victims, but the site has never been cleaned up properly. As a result of the disaster, people there continue to suffer from serious health problems such as blindness and breathing difficulties.

9/11 Terrorist Attack

On September 11, 2001, terrorists flew two planes into the World Trade Center in New York City. Two buildings collapsed, leaving more than 3,000 people dead. Some 40,000 brave people helped in the cleanup and rescue efforts. But the destroyed buildings had filled lower Manhattan's air with an estimated one million tons of hazardous dust. That dust included lead, asbestos, and other harmful materials. Thousands of people who helped out have since reported health problems, including rare lung-scarring diseases. Nearby city residents were put at risk as well. Experts expect to see a rise in asthma and other respiratory illnesses in the New York City area in the coming years.

California Wildfires

The California wildfires of the 2000s burned millions of acres of land up and down the West Coast. The fires also affected the quality of the air. Studies of the 2003 fires showed that the blazes had led to levels of particulate matter ten to twenty times higher than normal. This caused many people in the area to experience asthmalike breathing problems. There was also an increase in nose, eye, and throat irritations. The long-term effects of exposure to the forest-fire smoke are still unclear.

QUESTION TIME ?

When did people first start worrying about air pollution?

As long ago as the 1200s, people tried to limit how much coal could be burned and when, in order to limit the pollution from coal-burning fires. But in this century, major disasters focused attention on air pollution.

16

Firefighters were able to battle the California wildfires, but they could do little to stop the air pollution caused by the fires.

The Greenhouse Effect

Air pollution causes something known as the greenhouse effect. That's when heat gets trapped in the Earth's atmosphere.

Growing Amounts of Greenhouse Gases

It is normal for some heat to be trapped in our atmosphere. This is called **greenhouse effect**. A combination of water vapor, carbon dioxide, and methane gases act like a greenhouse, keeping the planet warm. But some of the Sun's heat bounces off the atmosphere and the Earth's surface and escapes into space. However, scientists have noticed that humans are adding to the amount of greenhouse gases in our atmosphere. Burning fossil fuels adds to carbon dioxide in the atmosphere. Decay in landfills creates methane gas that escapes into the air. These gases are keeping more heat in our atmosphere.

Temperatures on the Rise

In the past century, temperatures have risen almost 1 degree Fahrenheit (.56 degree Celsius). They are expected to rise another 2 to 6 degrees Fahrenheit (1.1 to 3.3 degrees Celsius) over the next one hundred years. This global warming, as it is called, could have devastating effects. The heat could warm the oceans and melt icy regions, causing severe flooding. In other areas, the heat will evaporate more water, causing water shortages.

Greenhouse Gases in Action

This diagram shows how greenhouse gases trap heat in our atmosphere. The Sun's energy travels through space toward our planet. Some of that energy is reflected back into space immediately, but the rest enters our atmosphere and warms our planet. Some of this heat escapes into space, but some of it is trapped. Air pollution has added more of these greenhouse gases to this layer, causing more heat to stay in our atmosphere.

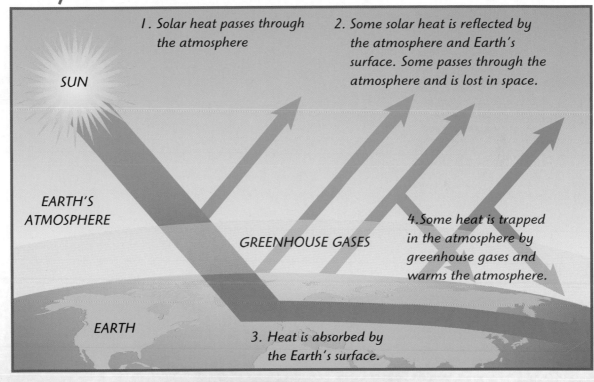

SUN

1. Solar heat passes through the atmosphere

2. Some solar heat is reflected by the atmosphere and Earth's surface. Some passes through the atmosphere and is lost in space.

EARTH'S ATMOSPHERE

GREENHOUSE GASES

4. Some heat is trapped in the atmosphere by greenhouse gases and warms the atmosphere.

EARTH

3. Heat is absorbed by the Earth's surface.

Pollution hangs over Sao Paulo, Brazil. Certain pollutants can trap heat in our atmosphere, causing global temperatures to rise.

Animals and Plants

Animals and plants suffer from dirty air, too. One big reason is acid rain. Acid rain results when dangerous chemicals combine with water in the air. This creates rain that is **acidic**, or very high in potentially harmful acids.

Acid rain hurts animals by polluting water sources.

Damage from Acid Rain

When **acid rain** falls, it soaks into the ground, plants, rivers, and lakes. This can affect animals and plants in many ways. Acid rain sometimes eats away at the protective coating on the leaves of a plant, which can kill the plant. Other times it can poison the water in lakes and rivers. Fish can become very sick and die. So can land animals that drink from these water sources. And it doesn't end there. People and other animals that rely on those plants and animals for food can lose a valuable food source.

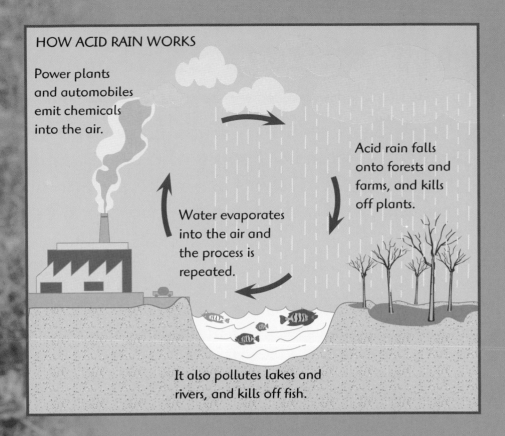

HOW ACID RAIN WORKS

Power plants and automobiles emit chemicals into the air.

Acid rain falls onto forests and farms, and kills off plants.

Water evaporates into the air and the process is repeated.

It also pollutes lakes and rivers, and kills off fish.

Dying Forests

Pollutants in the air can also be absorbed directly by plants. In many Eastern European countries, the emissions from coal plants have polluted the air badly. Hundreds of thousands of acres of forest have been killed off or badly damaged.

QUESTION TIME ?

What causes acid rain?

Acid rain is mostly caused by the burning of fossil fuels. When cars, energy plants, or anything else burns fossil fuels, the chemicals sulfur dioxide and nitrogen oxide are released into the air. There, they combine with water and then fall as acid rain, polluting water sources.

Air Heroes

People everywhere are finding ways to fight air pollution. Some are ordinary people who are making changes in their lifestyles. Others are leaders working to change attitudes and laws. Here are two "air heroes."

Al Gore

Since losing the 2000 presidential election, Al Gore has dedicated himself to an important cause: alerting people worldwide to the dangers of global warming. As a politician, Gore had been working on environmental issues since the 1970s. But after the 2000 election, he traveled around the world giving speeches about the dangers posed by the greenhouse gases, which humans are creating. He turned his speeches into a book and a movie, both called *An Inconvenient Truth*. Thanks to Gore's book and movie, millions of people now know about the possible consequences of global warming, and they are working to stop it.

The Tree Lady

During the 1970s, Wangari Maathai noticed that her country, Kenya, had some serious environmental problems. Forests were disappearing, soil was being eroded, or worn away, and there was a shortage of water. In 1977 she started the Green Belt Movement to help fix these problems. The movement encourages women in Kenya to plant and take care of trees. The plan quickly spread across Africa. Over the thirty-one years that the program has been in operation, thousands of acres of forests have been restored.

How do trees help protect against air pollution?

Trees are natural air cleaners. They actually filter pollutants from the air, including dust particles, and they store carbon dioxide. The forty million trees planted by Wangari Maathai and other African women have helped to make the air safer for all of us.

Wangari Maathai won the 2004 Nobel Peace Prize for her efforts to plant trees across Africa.

What Is Being Done?

Governments around the world are doing their part to reduce air pollution. Many have imposed strict air quality laws aimed at limiting air pollution.

Cleaning Up the Air

Over the past fifty years, people have made progress in preventing and limiting air pollution. In the United States, state and local governments enacted the earliest clean-air laws when they saw the damage from air pollution in their community.

Cleaner Cars

Automobiles have become much cleaner in recent years—it would take twenty of today's cars to match the emissions of just one car from the 1960s. And progress is still being made. In 2007 the United States passed new fuel efficiency rules for cars and trucks. By 2020 these cars will have to be 40 percent more efficient than they are today. This should lead to a big drop in the burning of fossil fuels.

The Clean Air Act

The U.S. government started researching the air pollution problem in the 1950s. The Clean Air Act of 1963 helped pay for programs to limit air pollution and encouraged the use of cleaner fuels. Later in the 1960s, amendments to this law set limits on harmful emissions from cars and trucks, factories, power plants, and some other businesses. More improvements followed in 1970, 1977, and 1990. These laws have led to amazing progress. Since 1970 harmful gas emissions have been reduced by fifty million tons. And carbon monoxide emissions have dropped by a third.

Dropping Air Pollution Levels

The graph below shows how carbon monoxide emissions dropped in the United States from 1970 to 2002. Carbon monoxide is just one of the harmful gases that have been reduced by air quality laws.

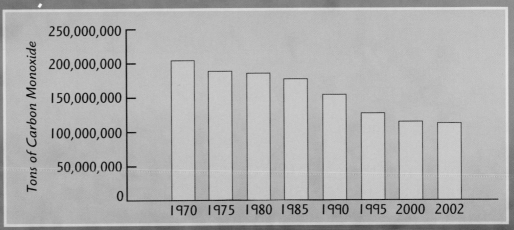

Source: U.S. Environmental Protection Agency, Office of Air and Radiation, 2002. Air Quality Trends Summary Report. January 2005.

Laws limiting air pollution have made it easier for all of us to go outside and enjoy the fresh air.

25

You Can Help, Too!

You've learned a lot about the problems caused by air pollution. But is there anything that you can do to help? Of course there is! There are many ways you can prevent air pollution, starting right in your own home.

Lights Out!

This is an easy one, but it's also easy to forget. When you leave a room, turn off the lights. If you're done with the computer, don't leave it on all night—shut it off. Cut back on leaving things on and you'll also cut back on electricity usage.

QUESTION TIME ?

What else can I do at home to prevent air pollution?

Most homes are heated by burning fossil fuels such as oil or natural gas. Turning down the heat means less burning and less air pollution. The U.S. Department of Energy suggests setting your thermostat at 68 degrees Fahrenheit (20 degrees Celsius) while you're awake and dropping it by 10 degrees to 15 degrees Fahrenheit (6 degrees to 8 degrees Celsius) when you're sleeping. This will also save money on fuel costs.

only
ALUMINUM
CANS
please!

Reduce, Reuse, Recycle

You've just polished off a refreshing bottle of water, so what do you do with the bottle? A lot of times people simply toss it in the trash. What a waste! Plastics can be recycled into everything from hammocks to buckets to pillows. By recycling, you're making sure that less new plastic needs to be made. That means less energy used and fewer harmful chemicals in the air. Reducing and reusing are great ideas, too.

Recycling is one way to keep items from ending up in landfills. Landfills can pollute the air with harmful gases.

ONLY
WHITE
OFFICE PAPER
PLEASE!

Getting Your Family Involved

There are many ways families are working together to save our air. Some are using alternative energy sources, such as wind and solar power, for their electricity. Some power companies let people choose the source of their energy.

Saving Energy at Home

Some families are switching to compact fluorescent light bulbs. These bulbs use a fraction of the energy that traditional bulbs use. Some appliances are also far more efficient than others. The U.S. government gives an "Energy Star" to appliances and other products that save on energy use and costs. Families look for this label to help the environment and to save money.

EYE-OPENER

How Solar Panels Work

Some people have solar panels installed on their homes, allowing them to get clean electricity and heat. Here's how one type of solar panel works. When the Sun is shining, the solar panels collect its energy (photons) and convert it into electricity (electrons). The energy is sent to a battery, which stores it until it is needed. Sometimes people even have enough energy leftover to sell it to the local power company!

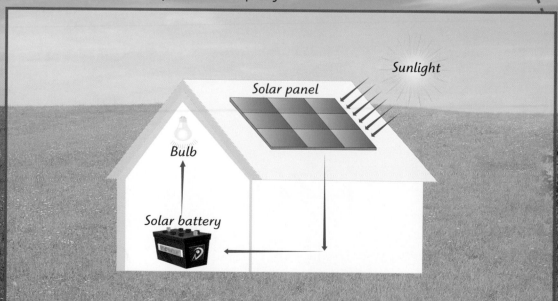

Fuel-Efficient Travel

One of the biggest ways that families are helping is through the cars they drive. Many families are opting for gas-sipping small cars or super-low emission hybrid vehicles instead of big gas-guzzlers. You can also share rides with others when you're headed to the same place. Or walk or bicycle when you're going short distances. You can enjoy the fresh air that you're helping to save.

Solar panels installed on homes can take the Sun's natural energy and use it to provide electricity and heat.

Glossary

acidic: High in acid, a substance that eats away at metals.

acid rain: Rain containing pollutants that make it high in acid.

asbestos: A material that was once used in insulation but has since been found to be harmful to the air.

asthma: A disease that causes the airways to tighten up and makes breathing difficult.

carbon monoxide: A colorless, odorless gas that is emitted when fossil fuels are burned.

emissions: Substances that are given off by a car, a factory, or another source.

exhaust: The steam and gases from an engine.

fossil fuel: Burnable materials, such as oil and coal, that are found in the ground.

fuel efficient: Using very little fuel. Some cars and trucks are more fuel efficient than others.

greenhouse effect: The trapping heat in the atmosphere by a combination of gases.

hybrid: A car or truck that is powered by both electricity and gasoline.

inhaler: A small device that lets you inhale medicine through your mouth.

methyl isocyanate: A chemical used in the production of pesticides and plastics.

nuclear power: An energy source that is created by using the nucleus of an atom.

particulate matter: Tiny bits of material that pollute the sky.

radon: A natural, harmful gas that sometimes builds up in homes.

smog: A thick mixture of smoke and fog.

zero-emissions building: A building that pumps no harmful materials (such as carbon dioxide) into the air.

Where to Find Out More

Books

- Donald, Rhonda Lucas. *Air Pollution*. New York, NY: Children's Press, 2002.

- Gore, Albert. *An Inconvenient Truth: The Crisis of Global Warming*. New York, NY: Viking, 2007.

- Petheram, Louise. *Acid Rain*. Mankato, MN: Bridgestone Books, 2000.

- Thornhill, Jan. *This Is My Planet: The Kids' Guide to Global Warming*. Toronto, Ontario: Maple Tree Press, 2007.

- Wilcox, Charlotte. *Recycling* (Cool Science). Minneapolis, MN: Lerner Publications, 2007.

Web Sites

- EcoKids:
  Created by Earth Day Canada, this site offers games, challenges, and information related to acid rain, air pollution, and other environmental issues.
  http://www.ecokids.ca/pub/index.cfm

- EPA Climate Change Kids:
  This U.S. Environmental Protection Agency site contains information on every aspect of climate change.
  http://epa.gov/climatechange/kids/

- The Know Zone: This site by the California Air Resources Board contains games, interactive learning experiences, and other information related to air quality.
  http://www.arb.ca.gov/knowzone/knowzone.htm

- Smog City: In this interactive game, you can see what effect certain types of activities have on the air quality of a city.
  http://www.smogcity.com/welcome.htm

Index